STEVEN
JOBS
Computer Genius

Laurie Rozakis

ROURKE ENTERPRISES,INC.
VERO BEACH, FLORIDA 32964

A Blackbirch Graphics Book.

Library of Congress Cataloging-in-Publication Data

Rozakis, Laurie.
    Steven Jobs / by Laurie Rozakis.
        p.   cm. — (Masters of invention)
    Includes bibliographical references and index.
    Summary: A biography of the inquisitive young computer genius who was one of the founders of Apple Computer company.
    ISBN 0-86592-001-X
    1. Jobs, Steven, 1955–   —Juvenile literature. 2. Computer engineers—United States—Biography—Juvenile literature. 3. Apple Computer, Inc.—History—Juvenile literature. [1. Jobs, Steven, 1955–   . 2. Computer engineers. 3. Apple Computer, Inc.—History.] I. Title. II. Series.
QA76.2.J63R69   1993
338.7'6100416'092—dc20
[B]   92-43268
                                                              CIP
                                                               AC

CONTENTS

LOOK OUT! GENIUS AT WORK!

"I was a loner for the most part."

Steven Jobs was a very curious little boy. As a result, he got into a lot of trouble. What would happen if you stuck a metal hairpin into an electrical socket? he wondered. He found out the shocking answer when he burned his hand badly. A few months later, when he and his friend were setting up a chemical laboratory, they drank some of the ant poison that they were using for their experiments. Steven had to be rushed to the hospital to have his stomach pumped.

What happened to this curious little boy? He put his curiosity to work and sparked the computer revolution that changed the way we do business—and the way we live. Along the way, he became a millionaire at age 23 and was worth more than $100 million by age 25.

Opposite: By the time he was 23 years old, Steven Jobs had become a millionaire and had helped to revolutionize the entire computer industry.

A Difficult Baby

Steven Paul Jobs was born on February 4, 1955, and was adopted soon after by Paul and Clara Jobs. Steven was a difficult baby. He had trouble sleeping and often woke up his parents with his crying. They finally hit upon the ideal situation: They bought him a record player to keep him busy. Later, as a small child, Steven played well with the children in his neighborhood. As the star of the home movies that he and his friends made, Steven liked dressing up in his father's raincoat and hat and playing a spy.

Steven's father had many different jobs. Paul was a machinist, a debt collector, and a backyard auto mechanic, among other things. Because of the frequent changes, the family moved a great deal. When Steven was five months old, the family left his birthplace of Palo Alto, California, and moved to the city of San Francisco—another temporary home.

When the finance company Paul worked for transferred him in 1960, he bought a house in Mountain View, 30 miles south of San Francisco. At the time, apricot trees covered the gently rolling hillsides. Soon, the hillsides would be covered with electronics factories and workshops. The area is called "Silicon Valley" and it is the world's largest producer of semiconductors and other electronic parts.

As a young boy, Steven had an active imagination. One of his favorite activities was dressing up as a spy and making home movies with his friends.

A Budding Inventor

From the beginning, Silicon Valley attracted engineers and other people who were deeply interested in new technical ideas and devices. Many of them brought home broken electronic equipment to tinker with in their garages. Driveways were lined with intriguing devices neighbors had created.

One day, Steven zoomed toward a carbon microphone that an electronics engineer had

Steven was always curious about how things worked. He used to spend hours with his friends, working on inventions and chemical formulas.

hooked to a battery and a speaker. The booming sounds fascinated him, but he couldn't figure out how the device worked. He raced home to ask his father about it. When Paul couldn't answer his son's questions, Steven did something that set a pattern for his life—he cornered the engineer and fired questions at him until he completely understood how the microphone worked. The engineer was so impressed with Steven that he set aside some time to teach Steven more about electronics.

At Cupertino Junior High, Steven's entry in the science fair was a rectifier that controlled alternating current. He had clearly listened carefully to the engineer's lessons.

The Loner

Despite his keen mind, Steven had a hard time in school. "I was a loner for the most part," he later said. His strong personality often came into conflict with authority. People resented the way he asked question after question until he had the answers he needed.

When Steven was nine years old, he was thrown out of a class for bad behavior. Not only did he misbehave, but he also refused to do his work. At her wit's end, his mother bribed Steven to do his lessons—it worked. He did so well in his studies that he skipped fifth grade, but he still acted up in class. "Steven is an excellent reader," his sixth-grade teacher reported. "However, he wastes much time during reading period."

He also had a hard time making friends, and the other kids teased him a lot. When he took swimming lessons, the other boys would snap wet towels at him. He finally decided to drop out of school. "He came home in the seventh grade and said if he had to go back there again, he just wouldn't go," his father remembered.

To ease their son's pain, Paul and Clara decided to move to Los Altos, California. Steven enrolled in Homestead High School. There, he would make the most important friendship of his life. It bailed him out of his loneliness—and changed the world.

Woz

Stephen Wozniak was five years older than Steven, an engineering whiz who invented wild gadgets. "Woz" was a loner, too, but he was so involved in electronics that he didn't feel lonely or set apart like Steven. With Woz's encouragement, Steven joined the electronics club at Homestead High.

In his spare time, Steven prowled through hobby shops, flea markets, and engineers' garages to find parts he and Woz needed for their electronic gadgets. How good was he at finding parts? One Saturday he was poking through a San Jose flea market for transistors. The next day, he took the transistors to an electronics shop and sold them for a profit!

Steven also showed his never-give-up spirit. Once, when he couldn't get a part at school that he wanted, Steven called the manufacturer—collect. He was astonished when his teacher explained that calling collect to ask for a favor was just not done. "You cannot call them collect," said Mr. McCollum, the electronics teacher. "I don't have the money for the phone call," Steven answered. "They've got plenty of money."

One day he even called Bill Hewlett, one of the founders of Hewlett-Packard, to get electronic parts. Along with the parts, Steven got a summer job—and a taste of his future. At Hewlett-Packard, Steven worked on the assembly line building computers. Fascinated, he tried to design his own computer, but he didn't know enough about computers yet.

Breaking the Law

Aside from fiddling with electronics, Steven and Woz loved to play practical jokes. Their pranks usually came close to being illegal. Once, for example, they built a fake bomb that terrified the school. Another time, they hung a tie-dyed sheet with an obscene gesture in the school. They even signed the sheet SWABJOB PRODUCTIONS.

One of their pranks was clearly illegal. Together, Steven and Woz created a "blue box" that allowed people to make free telephone calls. Woz had been first to stumble on an underground network of "phone phreaks," who used the device to call around the world.

It all started when Woz's mother read an article in *Esquire* magazine about the "blue boxes." The article explained how the boxes duplicated tones that the telephone company uses to put calls through. The outlaws used code names like "Cap'n Crunch" and "Dr. No" to protect their identities. The phone phreaks made free calls around the world, hooked into huge mainframe computers, and generally drove the phone company crazy. Knowing her son's fascination with electronic gadgets, Woz's mother gave him the article to read. That's all he and Steven needed. They were off.

Building the blue box was not a simple task. The telephone company had set up complex blocking systems. The boys called *Esquire* magazine, but the journalist refused to give out his information. After thoroughly searching the library, the boys found some general information on circuits.

Their first attempts were unsuccessful, but they finally worked out a method. The blue box ran on a 9-volt battery and had a small speaker. For their test run, Steven and Woz decided to call Woz's grandmother, who lived in Los Angeles. The box worked, but they got the wrong number.

The boys decided to contact the most famous phone phreak of all, Cap'n Crunch. How did he get his name? According to the legend, he had discovered a toy in a box of Cap'n Crunch cereal that created the necessary telephone tones to fool the switching device. Steven and Woz invited Cap'n Crunch over.

At age 15, Steven and his friend Stephen Wozniak created an illegal device that hooked into computers at the telephone company. Once it was perfected, the boys sold their creation to people who cheated the phone company.

He was a horrible disappointment—dirty, badly dressed, and skinny. But he did give the two boys lots of hints about using their illegal machine. His most important warning: Always call from a pay phone so the call can't be traced.

Soon after, the boys started selling their creation. Their venture lasted about a year. Woz and Steven said they never used the box to cheat the phone system. But they sold the boxes to customers who did.

THE REBEL

"Steven always had a different way of looking at things."

*S*teven's electronics teacher at Homestead High School, John McCollum, described Steven for *Time* magazine. "Steven always had a different way of looking at things," he recalled. After Steven graduated from Homestead High School in 1972, he looked at colleges as differently as he had looked at electronics.

He devoured stacks of college brochures. He prowled around Berkeley and Stanford, two large universities that were nearby. Both schools had excellent reputations, especially in the fields of science and electronics. In short, Steven became as deeply involved in college choices as he had in everything else that drew his attention.

What did he want in a college? The school
had to be up-to-date. Professors had to know
the latest ideas. It had to be tough, too—no
easy schools for him! In the end, Steven
picked Reed College in Portland, Oregon. This
choice made his parents unhappy because
Reed College was very untraditional. They
were so angry, in fact, that they refused to let
him enroll. Steven simply packed his bags and
announced that he was off. His parents
backed down. They drove him to the campus,
kissed him good-bye, and paid his school bills.

Peace and Love

Why did Steven pick Reed College? During
the 1970s, the school was a magnet for poets,
rebels, and other people searching for the
meaning of life. The most extreme rebels were
the "hippies." These were people who tried to
find out about themselves and create world
peace by farming, making crafts, and living in
groups called communes. The hippies set
themselves apart from others by their long hair
and unique clothing—bell-bottomed pants,
fringed leather vests, tie-dyed cotton shirts, and
beads. Reed College was at the center of the
rebellion, and Steven plunged in headlong.

Within weeks, he had thrown away his
shoes and grown a straggly beard to match his
longish hair. He gave up his dorm room and

became a "floater," living in different rooms around the campus. He rarely went to class. Instead, he spent his time talking with people and thinking about life. What are we doing here? he wondered. What is the purpose of life? he asked.

To find the answers, he read about the Eastern philosophies of Yoga, Buddhism, and Zen. As always, when Steven looked into something, he looked as deeply as he could. Buddhism sparked his interest because it stressed experience rather than intelligence.

Steven was determined to find out more. He and his friend Daniel Kottke hitchhiked to the Hare Krishna temple in Portland. After sharing the delicious vegetarian curry, they picked flowers to place on the shrine and bedded down for the night in the communal house. Steven liked the experience so much that he traveled back on many weekends.

The Dropout

A semester later, Steven dropped out of Reed College and decided to teach himself. He rented a room for $25 a month and spent his time reading, fasting, and thinking. Since he had left college, Steven's parents stopped giving him money.

He was flat broke, cold, and hungry. There was no heat in his room. To stave off

Steven dropped out of college to study on his own. Penniless and without a job, Steven spent his time reading Chinese philosophy and eating nothing but cereal.

the frigid Portland weather, Steven sat in his down jacket and tried to study *I Ching*, the Chinese Book of Knowledge. In desperation, he borrowed some money from the college. When that ran out, he took a job repairing the electrical equipment in the animal laboratory.

He was so poor that for three weeks he ate nothing but cereal. Soon, he looked like a skeleton. His friends were so worried about him that they invited him for meals as often as they could, but Steven wouldn't eat their meals.

He had decided that he could learn more if he ate nothing but fruit for two years. His skin turned different colors, depending on the fruit he was eating at the time.

In 1973, Steven heard about an Indian guru, or teacher, Neem Karolie Baba. He made up his mind to go to India to learn from him. His friend Dan Kottke wanted to go along, but neither young man could afford the trip. To get the money, Steven went back home.

Steven Works at Atari

One morning soon after, Steven spotted a classified ad in the *San Jose Mercury*. Atari, a video game company, was looking for someone to help design its video games. Atari had been started two years before by Nolan Bushnell, a pioneer in electronic arcade games. All Steven knew about Atari was that it had created a video game called Pong.

Excited about the job, he rushed right over to Atari's offices. He didn't even stop to clean up. The people at Atari were quite surprised by his wild, tangled hair; dirty bare feet; and skinniness. Talking a mile a minute, Steven convinced the supervisors at Atari that he could revolutionize the video-game business. Little did they know how right he was!

Steven plunged into his work at Atari with his usual enthusiasm. He was so involved

in it that he forgot to take care of himself. He
rarely combed his hair or took a bath. He
smelled so bad that he was asked to work at
night when no one else was around.

Sometimes Steven was insulting. People
got angry at his comments because he didn't
know much about electronics yet—certainly
nowhere near what most of the other workers
knew. But, "Steven was smarter than any-
body," as Woz later said. He learned very fast
because he kept asking questions. And he
improved many video games.

While Steven was working at Atari, he was
sent to Germany to fix some games that were
causing interference with television broadcasts.
Steven looked so messy that, when he arrived
in Germany, the engineers there were shocked
by his appearance. They sent a telegram to
Atari to make sure he was the right person.
Satisfied that he was, they put him to work.
He quickly fixed the problem. Then he went
off to India with Dan Kottke to see the guru
before returning to Atari.

Traveling Through India

The guru had died. To honor his memory,
Steven shaved his head, covered his body with
ashes, and sat up a whole night in an aban-
doned temple. Steven and Dan had no plans.
They decided to wander through India. As

A trip to India influenced Steven a great deal. When he returned home, his head was shaved, and he was wearing robes. Steven had also found a new sense of purpose for his life.

they traveled, Steven was shocked by the horrible living conditions that he saw. People were eating out of garbage cans and sleeping on the streets. In the face of all this misery, Steven decided that Thomas Edison had done more to improve people's lives than all the gurus who had ever lived.

When Steven returned home in the fall of 1974, people were startled by the way he looked and acted. "He was wearing saffron robes, had a shaved head, and was walking about a foot off the floor," noted Al Alcorm, Atari's chief engineer. But the look in Steven's eyes was the most surprising of all. Everyone could tell that something had changed.

TAKE A BYTE OUT OF THIS APPLE!

"We want to put a ding in the universe."

*M*eanwhile, Steven's friend Woz had gotten married and was working for Hewlett-Packard. In his spare time, he had created a small computer. To bounce his ideas off others, Woz hooked up with a group of young computer whizzes. They called themselves the Homebrew Computer Club. Steven began going to meetings in 1975.

Woz, like most of the club members, didn't think of selling his computers. He was happy just inventing them. "I wasn't too interested in making money," he recalled. "I just liked Homebrew. It became the most important part of my life."

When Woz hooked up his small computer to a television screen and a keyboard, Steven realized they were on to something big. How could they build and sell their home computer? he wondered. Steven attacked the problem with his usual determination. It didn't matter that he had no idea where his persistence would take him.

The History of Computers

The first modern electronic computer was invented at the University of Pennsylvania in 1946. The U.S. Army had commissioned the project. The ENIAC (Electronic Numerical Integrator and Calculator) had 18,000 vacuum tubes. It needed 18,000 square feet of floor space—about the size of a three-bedroom house. The transistor, invented in 1947, replaced vacuum tubes in radios, televisions, and the next generation of computers.

Soon, scientists linked tiny transistors to integrated circuits. But in the early 1970s, computers were still either very expensive toys or house-sized machines. They were useful only to the government, scientists, or the largest corporations. There were no personal computers.

All that changed on April Fool's Day in 1976, when Steven Jobs and Stephen Wozniak founded Apple Computer. Neither of them had any idea of the riches—and revolution—that lay ahead.

Steven wrote up a contract. He would be in charge of selling the computers. Woz would make them. The first problem: Where to set up shop? Steven and Woz couldn't possibly afford to rent space, so they decided to use Woz's cramped apartment. But Alice, Woz's wife, was not very happy. Her apartment had been transformed into a factory. Steven and Woz quickly trucked all the computer parts over to Steven's parents' house.

On April Fool's Day in 1976, Steven and Woz founded their own company, called Apple Computer. They set up their first office in Steven's garage.

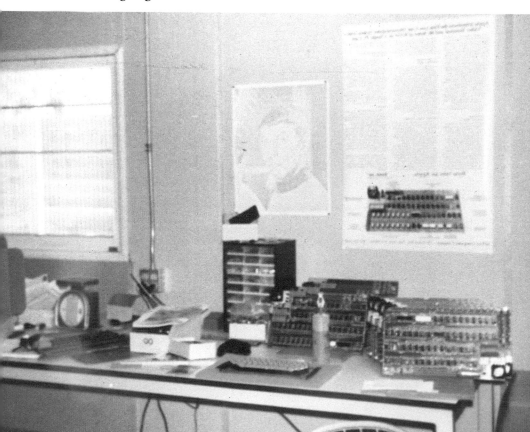

They crammed everything into a spare bedroom, filling the dresser with computer parts. The overflow flooded into Steven's room. And like magic, the entire house seemed to fill with computer parts. Metal solder dripped from every surface. Steven and Woz then moved everything into the garage. Steven's father pushed the car he had been repairing into the street. After all, he thought, cars could stand outside weather, but computer parts couldn't. Paul Jobs even put up walls and installed lights and a telephone line. The shop was born.

The second problem: How to get money? Steven looked everywhere for money to pay for parts and advertising. People were not willing to lend him large sums of money. After all, he and Woz were just a couple of young guys working in a garage. Besides, there was Steven's appearance to consider. He was thin, grubby, and often barefoot. Over and over, Steven was turned down. "You're too young," some said. "What experience do you have?" others asked. "No one will buy a home computer," still others sneered.

It seemed as if no one would give them a break. Steven decided to take drastic steps. He sold his most valuable possession—his Volkswagen microbus. Woz sold his most valuable possession—his calculator. This gave the partners $1,300. They were off!

Naming the Company

"You can't sell a computer without a name," Steven and Woz thought. What should their computer be called? No one could come up with a name. Finally, Steven thought back to a happy summer when he had picked apples in Oregon. "*Apple* would be the perfect name for the computer," he decided.

The designer drew an apple, but Steven said that it looked like a cherry tomato. What to do? He took a bite out. This bite is also a play on words. There is a computer term that sounds the same as *bite* but is spelled with a *y* instead of an *i*. A byte is a "binary digit," the

Steven and Woz pose proudly with one of their earliest computer boards for the Apple I.

smallest piece of information a computer can handle. Steven added bright rainbow stripes for good luck. The logo was born.

Now all that the company needed was a slogan. Steven decided on "Byte into an Apple." Everything was set—or was it?

The Big Break

The third problem: How to sell computers? Steven may have been young and scruffy, but he was very smart. He wanted people to think that Apple was a solid, established company rather than a partnership between two young guys working out of a garage. So, instead of having the mail delivered to his parents' house, he rented a post-office box. He also hired a telephone answering service. This way, the phone would be answered in a businesslike way. He hired intelligent people to help put together the computers so he and Woz could meet their deadlines.

Apple's big break came when the Byte Shop, a brand new computer store, ordered 500 Apple I's. Steven and Woz were shocked. This was the company's greatest and most important triumph. "Nothing in subsequent years was so great and so unexpected," Woz said. The Apple I cost $666.66 and was a huge success. About 600 machines sold, but the partners made almost no profit.

The first Apple I computer, built by Steven and Woz.

"The Apple I was really the first computer to address the needs of the hobbyist who wanted to play with software but could not build his or her own hardware," Steven later said. "It came with a digital circuit board, but you still had to go get your own keyboard, power supply, and television monitor. If you were a techie, the Apple I seemed to go ninety percent of the way."

Of course, if you weren't a techie, the Apple I went only 10 percent of the way. Many people who wanted to use the computer could not operate it. Dealers were saying, "I think I could sell ten times more of these if you would just put a case and keyboard around it." Steven and Woz thought, "How can we make Apple I better? What do people need from a computer? What do they want?"

A New Crop: Apple II

The answer came soon after. Strolling through the Palo Alto Research Center, Steven saw a new model computer. "It was as if, all of a sudden, the veil had been lifted from my eyes," he said. This computer had a mouse, a hand-held device that moves a pointer, or cursor, on a computer screen. It was just the inspiration Steven needed. He was now determined to build a "user-friendly" computer.

Once their first computers were introduced, Steven and Woz knew they would be a great success. They had no idea, however, just how big their little company would become.

Steven and Woz introduced the Apple II in 1977. This computer sold for $1,350 and was more like today's PC (personal computer). It had expansion slots so people could increase the computer's power, a floppy-disk drive, and a spreadsheet program.

The Apple II swept through businesses, small offices, and homes. Steven urged other companies to create software programs for Apple II. About 16,000 programs were written, including video games for kids and VisiCalc for accountants.

Steven knew that it wasn't enough to just invent Apple II. He had to sell it to people. He hired Regis McKenna, a top public-relations person in Silicon Valley. McKenna convinced A.C. ("Mike") Markkula to consider Apple.

Markkula had sold computer chips for a very large company, Intel, and knew a lot about the industry. By age 30, he was already a millionaire. Markkula was so impressed with Steven and Woz's creation that he invested $250,000 in the company and in May 1977, he became the chairman of the board. With his backing, Apple attracted other wealthy investors.

A major bank gave the partners a line of credit so they could buy supplies and pay later. Finally, Steven and Markkula hired John Sculley from Pepsi Cola to be the president. This later proved to be Steven's only mistake.

THE FALL

"Here at Apple, we have a chance to change the world."

On January 3, 1977, Steven, Woz, and Markkula formed the Apple Computer Company. The first order of business? Moving out of the garage. They set up the company in Cupertino, close to where Steven and Woz lived. The building was small, but it was huge compared with the garage.

At first, the company felt like a family. Everyone was excited about creating a brand-new product. People came to work early and stayed late. They felt useful and happy with themselves and their work. Apple Computer had a great new way of doing business, too. Employees felt that making a great computer was more important than making money. There was a relaxed feeling in the office.

People did things for others and worked together as a team. For example, everyone celebrated when customers walked in off the street and plunked down their money for an Apple II. There was a great uproar when Cap'n Crunch, the phone phreak, showed up one day to buy a computer. Steven even took long walks with people in the company to share his plans and dreams.

Workers felt their efforts were important. They were praised and got extra money and company stock for good work. People were excited to work at Apple.

Do It Right the First Time!

But Steven was a finicky boss. He demanded · that the inside of the machine look as good as the outside. Every line of solder on the circuit board had to be perfectly straight before he would approve a machine for sale. He told his workers that people were spending their life's savings on these machines, and they cared what they looked like on the inside.

The factory had to be spotless. Steven put on white gloves and walked through the factory, checking for dust. Dust could get into the machine and clog it up. "People should be able to eat off the factory floor," he told his workers. Steven thought they should take the extra few days or weeks needed to get the job done right. "We had a fundamental belief," Steven said, "that doing it right the first time was going to be easier than having to go back and fix it.

"You just make the best product you can," he explained, "and you don't put it out until you feel it's right." For example, he insisted on a one-year guarantee. Other people wanted only a three-month warranty. After a big fight, he won.

Some workers admired Steven for caring so much. Others, though, began to feel angry. They thought that he was poking his nose into their business and being too fussy.

Conflicts Develop Within Apple

Battles had begun. In 1979, division managers were appointed. Steven was not picked. He was furious, and he felt hurt at being closed out. Steven felt that Markkula and the board of directors had stabbed him in the back.

Workers were boiling mad, too. Some people had been given more money and stock than others. Those who got paid by the hour, for example, did not get any stock. Engineers, however, got a great deal. Hourly employees and engineers worked side by side. When hourly workers realized what was happening, they became angry. Good feelings in the company began to disappear.

On December 12, 1980, Apple Computer became a public company. This meant that the company sold its stock to anyone who wanted it, not just Apple employees. "Everyone wants a bite of Apple—Apple Computers, Inc.—but most will be lucky to get even a bit," The *Wall Street Journal* reported.

By the end of the day, Apple was worth $1,778 billion. This was twice the value of Pan Am, American Airlines, and United Airlines combined. People who had original stock became instant millionaires. There was much bitterness among those who did not do as well. Steven was worth $256.4 million. He was 25 years old.

The Macintosh Widens the Split

"How can we make the Apple II even easier to use?" Steven wondered. In 1979, Apple began to develop the Macintosh computer. Like an Apple II, it had a "mouse" to make usage simple. In 1982, Steven took charge of the project. "Macintosh is the future of Apple," he told his team.

Apple split into two companies. One half made the Apple II, while the other developed the Macintosh. People became even more jealous of each other. Things were bad for Apple outside the company, too. The market had changed.

**By 1980, at age 25, Steven's personal wealth exceeded $256
million. As part of Apple, Steven turned his attention to developing
new designs that would make his computers easier to use.**

Now, Apple was not the only company making personal computers. Many other companies—big and small—had jumped into the arena. There were so many companies that *Time* magazine didn't pick a Person of the Year in 1982. Instead, it put the computer on its cover. The most serious competition came from IBM, a giant firm. Pressure mounted at Apple, and tempers raged.

Black Wednesday

Rumors began to sweep through the company about big changes. People were afraid of saying or doing the wrong thing and losing their jobs. Soon after Apple became a public company, 41 of the employees were fired. The atmosphere was so gloomy that the day was called "Black Wednesday."

Markkula fired the president, Michael Scott. Steven took Markkula's job as chairman. The board of directors and Steven then hired John Sculley, the whiz from Pepsi Cola. The future looked bright, but things would get worse at Apple before they got better.

Steven Is Dismissed as Chairman

John Sculley had been a superstar at Pepsi Cola. A very powerful man, he knew how to get things done. He was determined to bring

peace to Apple Computers and to make it
number one again.

He dove right in. Up at 4:30 A.M., he
jogged five miles and was at his desk by 7:30.
He didn't leave until late at night. "Here at
Apple," he said in his first speech, "we have a
chance to change the world." He started by
changing Apple. Jobs were shifted, and computer prices were slashed. Still, Apple had a
terrible year. The stock dropped from $63.75
to $17.24 because people weren't buying
Apple computers. There were so many other
computers to choose from.

Steven had kept his hold on the company.
He was chairman, the largest stockholder, and
head of the Macintosh division. But soon after
Apple began selling the Macintosh, problems
were discovered with the machine. It did not
sell as well as Steven had predicted. Despite
all the problems, however, the company con-
tinued to pour money into the product. The
Apple II people were very angry. The split
between the two divisions grew even deeper.

John Sculley decided to reorganize the
Macintosh division and fire 1,200 people—and
Steven. The battle between Sculley and Steven
reached a crisis at the April 22, 1985, board
meeting. Sculley told Steven he would no
longer be in charge of Macintosh. Steven's
power was gone. "They've cut the heart out of
Apple," one employee said.

Steven poses for a portrait with Apple president John Sculley.
Soon after Sculley was hired, conflicts began to arise in the
management of the computer company.

The Lawsuit

Steven took a leave of absence from Apple. He wanted to think about his life. What direction would it take? During the summer of 1985, he looked deeply into himself. He spent hours listing things that were important to him. "Why not do it all over again?" he asked. "I can create a whole new company again!"

Steven met with Sculley to tell him about his new ideas. Sculley was very happy for Steven. He invited Steven to stay on Apple's board of directors and offered to have Apple finance 10 percent of the new company.

Things changed, however, when Steven invited people from Apple to join his new company. The board refused to give Steven any more money. They fired him as chairman and even filed a lawsuit against him. In the lawsuit, Apple claimed that Steven was stealing the company's secrets, taking the most important people, and using Apple technology. The news thundered through the computer industry.

Apple won the lawsuit. For three years, Steven could not hire any Apple employees or sell any products that might compete with Apple. Steven would even have to get Apple's approval for any product he sold.

Was Steven out? "Knowing Steven Jobs, I wouldn't bet against him," remarked a former co-worker.

WHAT'S NeXT?

*"We're going to change the way teachers teach
and students learn."*

*T*ime: 9:24 A.M.
Place: the Louise M. Davis Symphony Hall,
San Francisco. A select crowd of 3,000 awaits
the debut of the decade's most exciting new
product. "Can he do it again?" the crowd asks.
The music swells, and sprays of flowers begin
to perfume the air.

The curtain parts, and Steven Jobs, age 33,
unveils his latest creation—the NeXT computer.
The sleek black box, a cube about 12 inches
on a side, steals the stage. "AAAhhhhhhh!"
ripples through the crowd. The computer,
with its space-age design, is so beautiful that
the Museum of Modern Art asks Steven if it can
display it in its collection.

"We're unveiling a new architecture that will change the future of computing," Steven cries. "What is this new computer?" people wonder. "I asked people for their dreams, not their specs," he responds. The NeXT has 5,000 times more power than the Macintosh, Steven's last great computer. In fact, it is the most powerful computer on the market. The black cube uses the most advanced laser technology in the world. "We're going to change the way teachers teach and students learn," Steven shouts. What sets the NeXT apart from other computers?

First, it can juggle many tasks at a time. Students can do math and music on the same screen—at the same time. The sharp pictures on the screen stunned the audience. The "icons," symbols for programs and functions, are moving cartoons rather than the usual stiff outlines. They're funny, too. For example, the icon for getting rid of a file is a black hole, a swirling whirlpool. "The NeXT computer will create the next computer revolution," Steven declares.

NeXT is made in one of the most modern factories in the world. Circuit boards look as if they've never been touched by human hands. How can this be? The computer parts are built by supermodern robots. Steven bought some of the robots. When he couldn't find what he needed, he had the others built. He even had

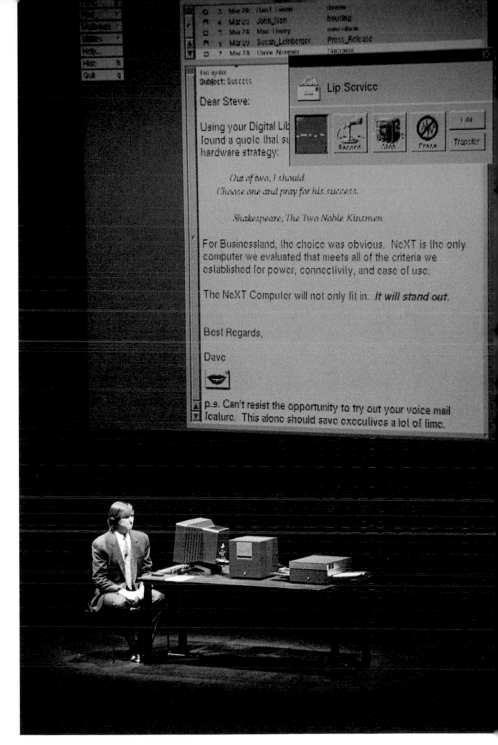

Steven does a live demonstration of his NeXT software in San Francisco. As president of NeXT, Steven was once again in the computer spotlight.

them painted all the same color so the factory would look better.

Steven gestures to the side of the stage, and a violinist emerges. She plays a classical duet. Who is her partner? The NeXT computer! The crowd roars its approval as the curtain goes down. Steven takes his bow to thunderous applause.

Steven had slipped from the public eye while he was creating NeXT. Once again, his picture is splashed across the front pages of newspaper and the covers of magazines.

Entrepreneur of the Decade

"It took us all of about five minutes to decide that our Entrepreneur of the Decade would be Steven P. Jobs," *Inc.* magazine declared in its April 1989 issue. "Granted, there are other entrepreneurs, a handful, who have enjoyed comparable success in the past ten years," they added, "but ultimately, their accomplishments pale alongside his."

Steven stands for a whole generation of pioneers on the frontier of technology. Not only was he building a company, but he was also experimenting with new ways of thinking about business itself. Newspapers, magazines, and television programs hail Steven for his creative spirit. "Part of the problem today is that we're not seeing enough mistakes," he

No matter what happens in the future, Steven Jobs will always be considered one of the most important innovators of the twentieth century.

says in an interview. "We're not seeing enough risk-taking," he adds.

Marriage and a Family

On March 18, 1991, Steven married Laurene Powell, a 27-year-old Stanford business student. What kind of wedding do you think Steven would want? He and Laurene were married at Yosemite National Park in central California. They had a very small, private ceremony, with fewer than 40 close friends and family members.

Steven had wanted to keep his wedding private, but news leaked out. For months, reporters followed him around to see what information they could get. They knew the wedding was getting close when he was seen at Tiffany's, a fancy jewelry store, shopping for a ring. He ended up spending more than $500,000 for it. "There goes one of Silicon Valley's most eligible bachelors," *Forbes* magazine reported when they saw him in the store.

In 1992, Steven and Laurene had a son. Steven was overwhelmed by parenthood. "It's a much bigger thing than I ever thought it could be," he said. "It changes your world. It's almost like a switch gets flipped inside you, and you can feel a whole new range of feelings that you never thought you'd have. It's sort of like if you never saw green and all of a sudden you have a child and you can see green for the first time."

The Tool Builder

"I'm a tool builder," Steven told reporters not long ago. "I'm proud of that. I love building tools and seeing what people do with them. Tools bring out the intellect and creativity in all of us. Humans are basically tool builders, and the computer is the most remarkable tool we've ever built. The important thing is to get them in the hands of as many people as possible."

Steven Job's picture was on the cover of *Time* magazine when he was only 26 years old. Today he is worth millions—about $210,000,000. Steven not only fulfilled his dreams, but he also created amazing products in the process. His products give us a peek at a bright and exciting future. How does Steven feel about all this?

"Years from now we're going to look back on what's happened with computers, and I think we'll see it as one of our most enduring contributions to civilization," he says. No matter how computers are judged, the jury is in on Steven Jobs: He is one of the most remarkable people of the late twentieth century and one of the most remarkable people that the business world has ever known.

GLOSSARY

byte A "binary digit," the smallest piece of information a computer can process.

floppy disk A thin, flexible disk with a magnetic surface, used for storing and retrieving information.

guru A spiritual guide.

hardware A computer's electronic or mechanical equipment. It includes the monitor (screen), keyboard, and computer.

icon A symbol on the computer screen that usually represents a file, folder, or disk.

laser Light energy that travels in a beam.

mouse A hand-held device that moves a cursor on a computer screen.

software Programs that direct a computer to do different functions.

spreadsheet A type of software that displays a work sheet, used for computing figures in budgets.

semiconductor A material that can conduct some electrical currents but not all.

transistor An electrical conductor developed in the 1940s.

vacuum tube An electrical conductor that was commonly used before the transitor was invented.

FOR FURTHER READING

Laron, Carl. *Computer Software Basics*. New York: Paragon House, 1985.

Nardo, Don. *Computers: Mechanical Minds*. San Diego: Lucent Books, 1990.

Turvey, Peter. *Inventions: Inventors and Ingenius Ideas*. New York: Franklin Watts, 1992.

Zomberg, Paul. *Computers*. Austin, TX: Raintree Steck-Vaughn, 1984.

INDEX

Photo Credits:
Cover: ©S. Kermani/Gamma Liaison; p. 4: Wide World Photos; p. 23: Apple Computer, Inc.; p. 25: Apple Computer, Inc.; p. 27: Apple Computer, Inc.; p. 28: UPI/Bettmann; p. 34: Wide World Photos; p. 37: ©Kashi/Gamma Liaison; p. 41: Wide World Photos; p. 43: NeXT, Inc.

Illustrations by Dick Smolinski.